TREASURE
HUNT
Activity Book

Jessica Mazurkiewicz

Dover Publications, Inc.
Mineola, New York

Copyright

Copyright © 2009 by Dover Publications, Inc.
All rights reserved.

Bibliographical Note

Treasure Hunt Activity Book is a new work, first published by
Dover Publications, Inc., in 2009.

International Standard Book Number

ISBN-13: 978-0-486-47042-9
ISBN-10: 0-486-47042-3

Manufactured in the United States by LSC Communications
47042307   2017
www.doverpublications.com

Note

Treasure hunters travel all over the world to find valuable items such as coins, statues, and jewels. In this exciting book, you will follow along as two treasure hunters visit deserts, jungles, and other parts of the globe in search of precious artifacts. Help them find what they are seeking as you complete crosswords and mazes, find what's different between two pictures, make matches, locate hidden objects, and many more fun activities. Solutions to the puzzles begin on page 54, but don't peek until you've tried your hardest! You can enjoy this little book even more by coloring in the pictures with crayons, colored pencils and markers, or felt-tip pens. Are you ready for adventure? Let's go treasure hunting!

Connect the dots from 1 to 30 to see an animal that treasure hunters ride on to cross the desert.

start

finish

Show this treasure hunter the path to take through the maze to reach the treasure room hidden below.

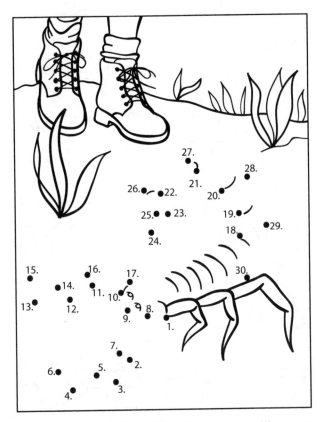

Connect the dots from 1 to 30 and you will see an animal that a treasure hunter is careful to avoid!

Draw a line to connect the scarab statue at the top of the pyramid to a matching statue.

The treasure hunter needs to find the five ancient artifacts shown above. Look for them in the picture of hieroglyphics on the opposite page.

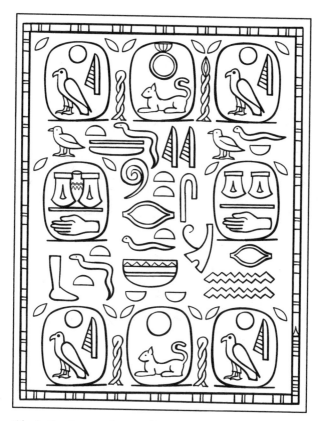

Circle the five ancient artifacts hidden in the picture.

Look carefully at the two pictures of the treasure hunter swimming to the sunken treasure chest.

Circle the four things that make this picture different from the one opposite.

Can you find the twin of the priceless statue in the center? Draw a line to the statue that looks exactly the same.

12

Circle the three crocodiles whose heads are peeking out of the river. Then the treasure hunter can cross the water safely.

13

Here are two pictures of treasure maps. They look the same, don't they?

Now find and circle the four things on this treasure map that make it different from the one opposite.

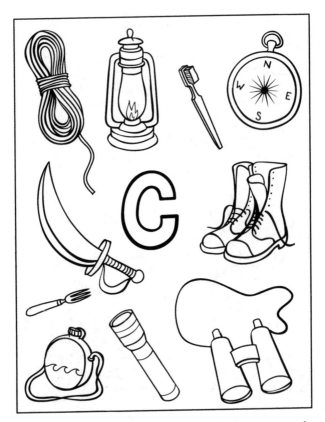

Here are some objects that a treasure hunter travels with. Circle the things that begin with the letter "C."

Help guide the treasure hunter's ship through the choppy seas to the treasure island.

The treasure hunter must find the five ancient artifacts shown above. Look for them in the picture on the opposite page.

Circle the five ancient artifacts hidden in the picture.

Six precious artifacts are floating in the water above this diver. Look carefully and you can find them in the picture on the opposite page.

Circle the six precious artifacts hidden above.

Connect the dots from 1 to 16 to see how this treasure hunter reaches the ancient ruins.

Find and circle the letters D, I, A, M, O, N, and D hidden in the jungle ruins.

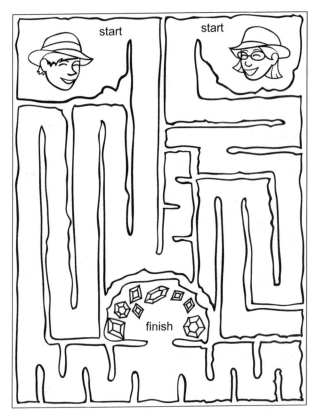

Only one of these treasure hunters knows which path
leads to the jewels. Complete the maze and find out
which hunter reaches the prize.

24

Valuable treasure is locked in the chest shown above. To open the chest, circle the key that matches the key shown in the oval.

Help the treasure hunter find the five ancient artifacts shown above. Look for them in the picture on the opposite page.

Circle the five ancient artifacts hidden in the picture.

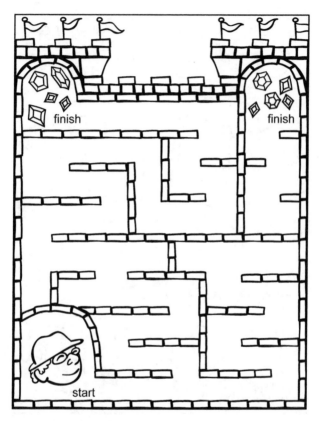

finish

finish

start

Only one path will take the treasure hunter through the castle to the riches at the end. Complete the maze and find which prize he will reach.

28

Two of these precious crowns are exactly alike. Find and circle the two crowns that match.

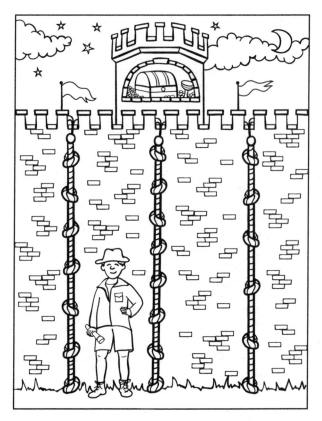

There are two ropes for the treasure hunter to climb to reach the tower. Circle the rope that has the fewest knots.

30

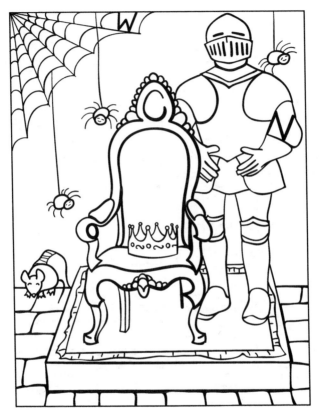

Find and circle the letters C, R, O, W, and N. They are hidden in this ancient throne room.

Look carefully at the images of the ancient temple on these two pages.

Now circle the six things that make this picture different from the picture on the opposite page.

These eight warrior statues look the same, but only two match. Find and circle the two matching statues.

Help the treasure hunter find the letters J, A, D, and E. Circle these hidden letters in the picture.

The letters G, O, L, and D are hidden in the cave. Find and circle all four letters.

Find and circle the two gold coins that are exactly the same.

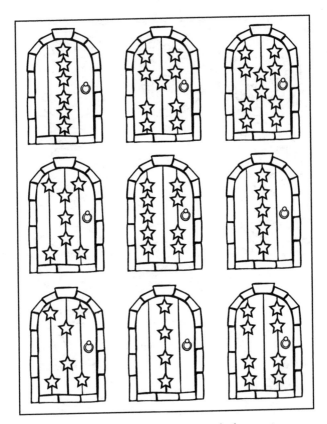

The door with the most stars on it has a treasure behind it. Circle the door that has the most stars, and the fabulous treasure is yours!

38

Find the shortest path through the abandoned mine, and you will help the treasure hunter reach the exit.

Some ways that a treasure hunter uses to travel are shown above. Circle only the ones that begin with the letter "H."

Find and circle the three snakes in the picture, and then the treasure hunter will be able to safely choose a vine to climb!

Look carefully at the two pictures of the treasure hunters escaping from a volcano.

Now find and circle the six things that make this picture different from the one on the opposite page.

Help the treasure hunter find the five ancient artifacts shown above by looking carefully at the picture on the opposite page.

44

Find and circle the five ancient artifacts hidden above.

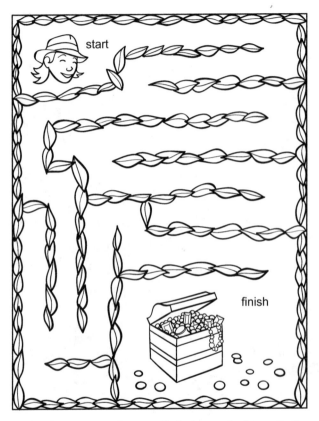

start

finish

Help the treasure hunter find the path through the jungle maze to reach the treasure at the end.

46

Look at the items surrounding the treasure hunter. Circle three things that he might use to search for treasure.

Treasure hunters try to avoid dangerous animals as they travel. Draw a line from each animal on the left to its footprint on the right.

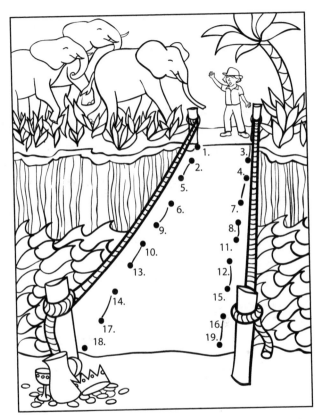

1.
2.
3.
4.
5.
6.
7.
8.
9.
10.
11.
12.
13.
14.
15.
16.
17.
18.
19.

Connect the dots from 1 to 19 to make a bridge that the treasure hunter can use to escape from the elephants.

The six golden coins that the treasure hunter has dropped are hidden in the picture on the opposite page. Can you find them?

Circle the six golden coins that are hidden along the jungle path.

Here are two pictures of the treasure hunter exploring ancient ruins in the forest.

Look carefully at this picture. Find and circle the six things that make this picture different from the one on the opposite page.

SOLUTIONS

page 4

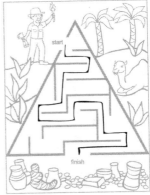

page 5

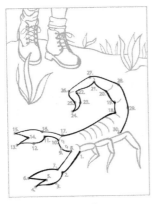

page 6

page 7

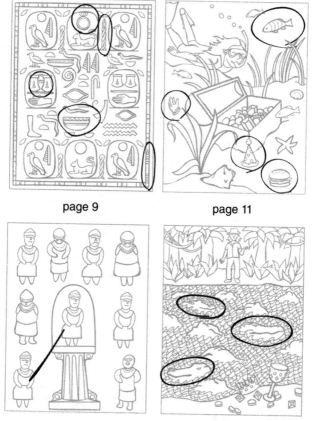

page 9

page 11

page 12

page 13

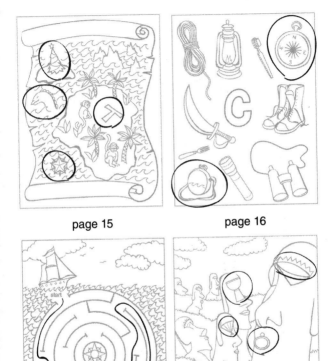

page 15

page 16

page 17

page 19

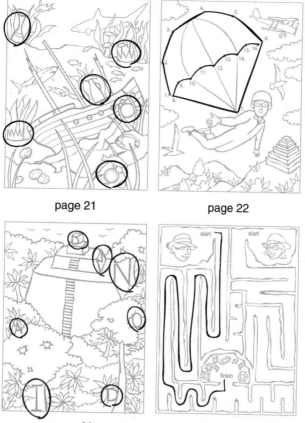

page 21

page 22

page 23

page 24

58

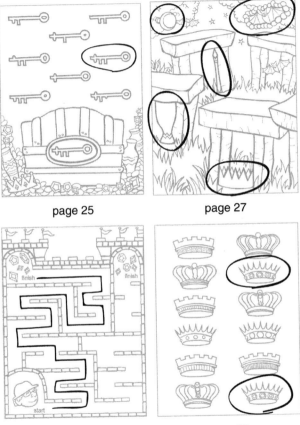

page 25

page 27

page 28

page 29

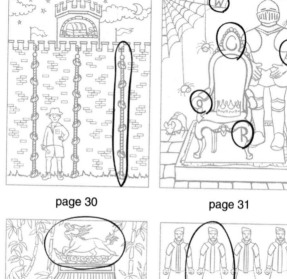

page 30

page 31

page 33

page 34

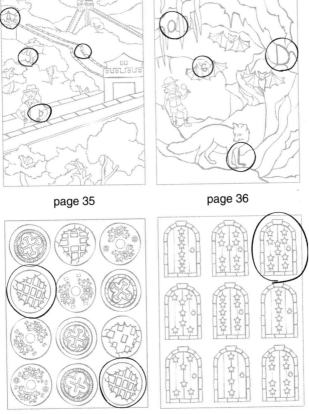

page 35

page 36

page 37

page 38

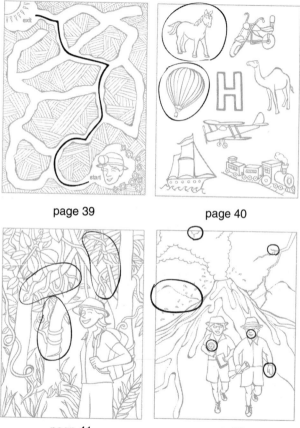

page 39

page 40

page 41

page 43

page 45

page 46

page 47

page 48

page 49

page 51

page 53